Mysterious Sphinx

or

The Secret Word

Professor Hilton Hotema

ISBN #: 978-1-68365-073-7

2017 Edition Editor: Prizgar G.
Print Coordinator: Prizgar G.
Book Cover Design: Ras Tzaddi Wadadah II

The Mysterious Sphinx

Or

The Secret Word

By

Prof. Hilton Hotema

A startling expose Showing how a symbol of the ancient masters Evolved into the God of Christianity.

Pious Fraud

In the 4th Century A.C., the church fathers Stole the Secret Word of the Ancient Masters, Which symbolized the FOUR COSMIC PRINCIPLES OF CREATION, changed the meaning of the Secret Word to indicate their God, then Destroyed the Ancient Mysteries and the Ancient Literature to hide their crime, and Slaughtered more than seventy million people To make the world believe in the Fraud that Evolved into Christianity.

In the John Gospel, the Process of Evolution changed the Secret Word to God -- The Word was in the beginning; and The Word was with God; and The Word was God.

Table of Contents:

Chapter 01 — The Great Fraud 01
Chapter 02 — Science of Man 04
Chapter 03 — Artificialism 05
Chapter 04 — Freedom of Mind 06
Chapter 05 — Words 08
Chapter 06 — Initiation of Anointed Iesous 10
Chapter 07 — Origin of Sphinx 12
Chapter 08 — Ancient Symbology 14
Chapter 09 — Biblical Description of Sphinx 15
Chapter 10 — The Ancient Masters 16
Chapter 11 — Ancient Wisdom 18
Chapter 12 — Four Great Principles 20
Chapter 13 — Je-Ho-Vah 21
Chapter 14 — The Secret Word 24
Chapter 15 — The Tarot 27
Chapter 16 — Psychology & Metaphysics 47
Chapter 17 — Initiation 49
Chapter 18 — Four Fixed Signs 55
Chapter 19 — Angelic Plan 56
Chapter 20 — The Great Pyramid 59
Chapter 21 — Four Departments of the Body 61
Chapter 22 — Twelve Zodiac Signs 63
Chapter 23 — Cosmic Chemistry 64
Chapter 24 — The Guard 66
Chapter 25 — Animal Sacrifice 67

Chapter 26 — The Consuming Fire **70**
Chapter 27 — The God of the Earth **72**

Chapter 1 — The Great Fraud

The greatest fraud ever invented; the greatest fraud the world has known. God, the creator of the world, and his son Jesus, the savior of the world.

Of this Jesus, Pope Leo X (1475-1521) said: "How well we know of what a profitable superstition this fable of Christ has been for us". (Doane's Bible Myths, p.438)

And the Son is greater than the Father. Jesus Personifies the Sun of the Universe, while his Father is only the personification of an Ancient Symbol.

The ancient Hindus called the Sun Kris. Their Krishna was a personification of the Sun, and they worshipped him as such. The English added "T" to Kris, making it Krist, then changed the spelling to Christ to deceive the masses. Similar fraudulent tricks were used by the church fathers in the invention of their God.

The Ancient Masters had an ingenious Symbol that embodied the Four Principles of Creation. The Symbol was designated by a name of Four Letters, and the name was never pronounced. It was always spelt. So this Secret Word was called the Ineffable Name; and it became the "Lost Word" of Freemasonry.

The Symbol the church fathers stole when the Roman State Church was founded; and they personified it, and called it God, creator of the world and the Father of the gospel Jesus.

It has been quite easy for the Free-thinkers and the Truth-seekers to dispose of the fabulous Jesus to the satisfaction of all thinking persons with an open mind. But disposing of the church God in a convincing manner has been a much more difficult task.

Those who have tried it have failed to accomplish much because they did not know where the church got its God, nor what he represented when the church found him. So they resorted to ridicule and caricature, which is not the kind of evidence that will convince many, nor cause many to change their opinion.

We shall describe the Ancient Symbol which the church God represents, and show how carefully the basic knowledge of this great Symbol was destroyed by the church fathers in order to provide better safety for their God.

The world has always had two leading groups of men, divided into -- 1.The Truth Seeker who sought to free their brothers and fellows from darkness and give them Light, and -- 2. The Tyrants who sought to enslave the masses by destroying Light and keeping them in darkness.

Evidence of this struggle down thru the ages appears in the Bible, and it is in progress at this hour. The Truth Seekers striving to enlighten the masses and lead them out of darkness and the Tyrants striving to crush the Masters and keep the masses in darkness and slavery.

The Ancient Masters developed a series of symbols in which to conceal their discoveries of the mysteries of Life, one of which is the Sphinx and another being the Caduceus.

The Sphinx is the subject of this work. Those interested in the mysteries of Life symbolized by the Caduceus will find that amazing information in our work titled The Magic Wand.

Symbolism is the art of expressing or representing Cosmic Powers, Principles, Processes, and Products by the use of signs and emblems.

A symbol may represent an object, a figure, a type -- as the lion is the symbol of fire and fierceness; which is the symbol of purity; a scepter, the symbol of power; the All-Seeing-Eye, the symbol of Omniscience.

For the reasons stated, the esoteric teachings of the Masters were conducted by means of symbols, parable, fables, fiction, and allegories. Symbolism was also used by the Masters to meet a read need -- as *"Words there are none. For the heart's deepest desires."*

The Bible confuses the clergy and the layman because it is a book of symbol and allegory, which can be interpreted only by him who knows the substances of the Masters' teachings and is an expert in astrology, biology, psychology, physiology, anatomy, and all true sciences related to Cosmic Principles and Processes as they are individualized and manifested in the Microcosm.

To interpret correctly the symbols of allegories of the Masters requires that we understand the substance of their teachings. The question of whether or not their teachings were always right and correct is irrelevant and immaterial.

The Bible is a book of these symbols and allegories but with many spurious interpolations and distortions, as the church fathers in their attempt to make the Bible say what the Ancient Masters did not teach, sought to muddy the water and confuse the reader.

Chapter 2 — Science of Man

The teachings of the Masters were based on the Science of Man, and Man is the subject of the Bible.

But as the church fathers prepared their Bible from Ancient scriptures, they filled their book with distortions and spurious interpolations, in their effort to make the Bible relate to their anthropomorphic God and their Kingdom of Heaven.

It was the work of Art to furnish the suggestion for the Mind, and those who could furnish it were the artists. Thus was developed the Art of Symbolism, which was the Masters' efforts to produce from their discoveries the cosmic phenomena they saw in Nature.

If the Art of symbolism were traced to its origin, it would disclose facts and truths more profound than modern scientists could comprehend. For instance, the simple crossing of two lines, or of two triangles, are symbolical expressions more fundamental than can be found in any modern art gallery.

In order to commune with Cosmic Powers and Principles, Master Artists retired into the Silence, either consciously or otherwise. This is a state of total relaxation, a release of the Senses and the Mind. In that state the Adepts do their great work and receive their strange flashes from what they see in Nature.

To be asleep is to be in Silence, and often the sleeper has strange and marvelous dreams.

Art is a thing apart. The Conscious phase of mind is the draftsman, or the Medium of Expression, while the Subconscious or Superconscious phase of Mind is the Creator.

Chapter 3 — Artificialism

As man becomes more civilized, the more artificial and decadent he becomes. He forsakes the natural and loses his self-sufficient creative powers. He then invents a Culture to replace his lost faculties.

So-called cultures spring from the schools and churches invented by Tyrants and Despots to control the Mind and to replace the natural abilities and propensities that man loses by being artificialized and regimentized. His natural instinct is semi-dormant, and his higher intuitive, noetic consciousness is inactive. He is deceived by the popular slogan: "Better schools build better communities.

The Ancient Masters, living with Nature, free of artificialization and regimentation, being "uncivilized" as the Tyrants and Despots would say, they were expert naturalists and skillful symbolists. Their Mind was free of all control, and their faculties were not limited by the rules of schools and churches. They made great discoveries in the mysteries of Life and communicated the essence of their discoveries in mystic symbols. Stukely says, "The first learning of the world consisted chiefly of symbols. The wisdom of the Ancient Masters was symbolic."

The legends of the Ancient Mysteries are parables, and a parable is only a spoken symbol. By its utterance, says Adam Clarke, "spiritual things are better understood and make deeper impressions on the attentive Mind."

Chapter 4 — Freedom of Mind

Symbology favors independence and promotes mental development. Only a symbol can free man from the slavery words and formulas, and permit him to rise to the possibility of thinking freely -- a function prohibited by institutions and organizations, the result being Mind Control and Mental Slavery.

Only by the use of Symbols can we penetrate deeper into the secrets of Life, into those facts and truths which the schools and churches so readily transform into monstrous delusions. When we attempt to express them in direct words without the aid of symbolical allegories, we fail.

The Silence which the Ancient Mystery schools imposed on the Initiates and Disciples finds its justification in this fact. An effort of the Mind is required for the understanding of occult secrets. They can illuminate the Mind internally but cannot serve as a theme for rhetorical arguments.

Occult knowledge cannot be expressed and transmitted orally or in writing. Only by profound meditation can it be acquired. It is necessary to penetrate deeply into the Inner Man, the Kingdom Within, to discover it. Those who seek it outside of themselves are on the wrong path and lost.

It is in this sense that we must understand the words of Socrates, "Know Thy Self." For the Magic Kingdom is within (Luke 17:21) and there must we look and search to know Man as he is and not as science pictures him.

Of the ignorance of science as to living things, the great Carrel said: "Those who investigate the phenomena of Life are as if lost in an inextricable jungle, in the midst of a magic forest, whose countless trees unceasingly change their place and their shape. These investigators are crushed by a mass of facts which they can describe but are incapable of defining in algebraic equations". (Man The Unknown, p.1)

Chapter 5 — Words

Scholastics bring to the ultimate analysis words only -- something entirely artificial and related to the physical realm.

By its very nature, a word is an instrument of paradox. Any theme can be defended by means of argumentation. This is so because every discipline deals not with realities reaching our consciousness by themselves, but only with their oral representations, with the fantasies of our Mind, which often allows itself to be deceived with the false coin of our thoughts and senses.

Pure Truth cannot be confined to any formula. From this it follows that, in a certain sense, every word is false. The Inner side of Thought, its fundamental Spirit, eludes us. And that is the Spirit which continually reveals itself and yet never allows itself to be seen, except in its reflections only.

Our sense of sight deceives us. The Sun does not rise. We do not see the sun, moon, and stars. These bodies which we do see are cross-sections of spirals. What we see does not correspond to reality. We are deceived by our senses.

What appears as the Sun is a focus of the airy layer of the physical plane of the physical world and focuses matter which comes into it from the (1) fiery, (2) airy, (3) watery, and, (4) earthly layers upon and into the earth layer. It precipitates this four-fold substance with the aid of the moon to the other earth crust (p.396).

The moon is fluid-solid, not so solid as the earth crust, and is a mass or body in the watery layer. It screens, filters, magnetizes, demagnetizes, modifies, and adjusts the substance that flows from the Sun to the Earth crust and from the Earth crust back to the Sun (p.581).

As we do not see what we think we see, it follows that when necessary to express transcendental ideas, we are forced to have recourse to figurative language, to the use of symbols. So it is impossible to eliminate symbols and allegories. This is not a matter of choice; for very often there is no other way of making oneself understood.

That is the reason why Pure Thought cannot be transmitted orally. That is the reason why science is now "lost in an inextricable jungle", as the great Carrel wrote. Why science is wandering "in the midst of a magic forest, whose countless trees unceasingly change their places and their shape".

Pure Thought must be clad with something the human mind can grasp and understand. But this covering is always transparent to him who knows how to see, how to hear, and how to think.

In Revelations the scribe said five times in the 2nd and 4th chapters -- "He that hath an ear, let him hear," -- indicating that the messages were in fabulous form and not in the literal language.

In the realm of Symbolism, one must not attempt to be too exact. Symbols represent ideas which, by their very nature, are difficult to embrace, and which are quite impossible to reduce to scholastic definitions.

Chapter 6 — Initiation of Anointed Iesous

For various reasons, the deeper secrets of Life discovered by the Masters were never given openly to the masses. Pure Thought cannot be received by the unprepared Mind. The Light of Pure Thought is too strong for the unprepared man's eyes, especially when he sees it for the first time.

There is terrible power and danger in new ideas that appear unexpectedly. There must first be a course of training and preparation, such as that which was required of candidates for Initiation on the Ancient Mysteries. That is the reason why the scribe made his Jesus say, "All men cannot receive this saying, save they to whom it is given". They are prepared. (Matthew 19:11)

That is another reason why the great secrets of Life were preserved for posterity in symbols and fables, puzzling to the exoteric but plain to the esoteric. They were explained in detail in the Ancient Mysteries to those who proved by rigid test that they were prepared and worthy to receive the secret Wisdom.

We behold this trembling candidate for Initialization, symbolized in the Bible as a Lamb standing in the midst of the Masters, as if it had been sacrificed -- so presented to make the gullible Christians think the Lamb represented the gospel Jesus (Revelations 5:6). The original title of Revelation was the Initiation of Anointed Iesous"-- the last word referring to one "who had been tried, tested, and prepared for Seership".

With its Seven Horns and Seven eyes, the Lamb also represents the Seven Sense Powers of Consciousness of Seership. The Seven Horns symbolize the Seventh Sense Power of Action, while the Seven Eyes symbolize the Seventh Sense Power of Perception.

In the Ritual of Initiation, the candidate was taught by the Masters how to resurrect and activate the Seven Great Nerve Centers (Chakras) of his own body, about which modern science knows almost nothing; and by this process, the candidate was raised up to a higher plane of Consciousness.

The Evidence of such activation is the Power of Seership. But that statement was not so translated from the Greek by the church fathers. In their Bible, they made it falsely read: "For the testimony of Jesus is the Spirit of Prophecy". (Revelations 19:10)

That statement refers to the resurrection of the semi-dormant glands of the sixth and seventh sense powers of man, called Seals in the Bible; and the evidence of their resurrection or activation is the power of Seership -- that strange power of the senses which raises man from the common five (five loaves -- Matthew 14:14) to the rare seven (seven loaves -- Matthew 15:34) sense plane of consciousness.

As we see, these sense powers are symbolized in the Bible by "loaves", and the "S" was capitalized in the Seven, but the "f" was not in the five. The Bible does not treat God and Heaven, as the church teaches, but of Man, his Redemption by his own work, and the response of his body.

By the term "Ancient Masters", we mean the great men who lived ages before Moses and Solomon and from whose teachings Moses and Solomon received their learning. The so-called Wisdom of Solomon consisted of what he had learned from the teachings of these Masters.

Chapter 7 — Origin of the Sphinx

The oldest and greatest of the Ancient Symbols that have come down to us is the mysterious Sphinx. The Sphinx is the Greek name of this symbol and means to bind or draw tight, to squeeze. The Egyptians call the Sphinx Hu, or Neb.

"The type perhaps originated in Egypt," says the encyclopedia, "and was borrowed from there by Greek art." As the figure of the Sphinx was founded more commonly on tombs, Milchhofer inferred that the Sphinx was a symbol of death.

The encyclopedia says that in mythology of Ancient Egypt, the Sphinx represented the solar deity, Ra, and adds: "All nations of antiquity seem to have held these monstrous beings of various shapes and forms (Sphinx) as objects of awe, compelling adoration and worship."

We shall understand this "awe" and "adoration" of the Sphinx when we learn later that the Sphinx symbolized in the Ancient world. The early church fathers knew, so they destroyed the ancient literature that told the story. They then feigned ignorance when they prepared the literature that gives us a history of the ancient world.

The Arabian Traveler and historian Abdullatif (1162-1231 A.D.), in referring to the Sphinx at Gizeh, said: "In spite of its enormous size, everything was in proportion to nature... In a face of such colossal size, how the sculptor could have been able to preserve the exact proportions of every part, seeing that nature presented him with no model of a similar colossus, or anything at all comparable". (DeStacy's trans. p.180).

This Sphinx is carved from the solid rock upon which it rests.

We have consulted two encyclopedias, the Britannica and the Americana, and condensed above all the important information they contain on the Sphinx, showing that the authors of these works knew no more about the true symbology of the Sphinx than the man in the moon.

Chapter 8 — Ancient Symbology

The authors of modern works on ancient symbology seem to know but little of the inner meaning of these symbols. About a century ago, there appeared a large work, in two thick volumes, by Thomas Inman, M.D., entitled Ancient Faiths Embodied in Ancient Names This was a work on symbolism. In a subsequent work on the same subject, Inman said, "In this work, the Author is obliged to confine himself to the explanation of symbols and cannot launch out into ancient and modern faiths, except insofar as they are typified by the use of certain conventional signs."

Of all the symbols listed in this later work, Inman neglected to include the two most important ones, viz, and the Sphinx and the Caduceus. No doubt this was because they were too deep for him, and he could not find them described in any ancient literature, as the church fathers destroyed it. Of the Sphinx, the encyclopedia Americana (1938) says: "A mythological monster variously described. . .The Sphinx, in the mythology of Ancient Egypt, represented the solar deity, Ra." This is true, but we shall find as we proceed that the Sphinx represented much more than just the solar deity.

We quote again from Abdullatif: "At a little more than an arrow's flight from the pyramids is a colossal figure of a head and neck projecting from the sand; the name of the figure is "Father of Terrors"."

Thus we observe that as late as 1231 A.D., this gigantic figure was still buried in the sand clear up to its neck, just as the early Egyptians had found it and were at a loss to know what it represented.

Chapter 9 — Biblical Description of Sphinx

No enlightening interpretation of the Sphinx appears in the Bible, although it was hoary with age before the books of the Bible were written, and the references to the Sphinx it contains are wild and misleading.

Ezekiel saw a whirlwind come out of the north, a great cloud, and a fire infolding itself ... and out of the midst thereof came the likeness of four living creatures. Then he proceeds to give a sensational description of the sphinx, and has it mixed up with the Zodiac, the description of which is just as sensational. (Chap. 1:4, 5, 15-21).

Daniel saw strange things in a vision. The four winds of heaven strove upon the great sea (Mediterranean), and four great beasts (Sphinx) came up from the sea. Then he gives a sensational description of the Sphinx.

In Revelation, four beasts appear in the midst of the throne and round about the throne. The first was like a lion, the second like a calf, the third had man's face, and the fourth was like a flying eagle (4:6,7). Just another description of the Sphinx.

Why does the Sphinx seem to play such an important part in the ancient scriptures? That is what we are going to learn.

Chapter 10 — The Ancient Masters

Tens of thousand of years ago, the Lemurian Masters invented symbols to conceal and represent their discoveries of the mysteries of Life, using them as charts in the work of teaching their disciples and followers. Their descendants left a copy of one of the greatest of these symbols in Egypt in the form of the Sphinx.

According to legend, Hermes Trismesgistus brought from Atlantis the sacred knowledge concealed in the Zodiac, and the epic of the Seven Days and Seven Nights of Creation. The context of this epic, in a badly distorted manner, appears in the Bible, chapters one and two of Genesis.

The original sacred Seven of the Lemurian Masters represents the Seven Cosmic Orders of the Four Great Principles of the Universe, consisting of Fire, Air, Water, and Earth, and strangely symbolized by the Sphinx.

When the earliest Egyptians settled in the Nile Valley, they found the Sphinx and Great Pyramid almost completely buried in the sand. The Sphinx is 189 feet long, carved from solid stone, and is one of the greatest of the ancient symbols. The Sphinx of Egypt is far older than historical Egypt; older than her gods; much older than the world suspects.

When Constantine founded the Roman State Church in the 4th century, that abruptly ended Classical Antiquity, and his army of fanatical destroyers battered and broke the nose of the Sphinx, and would have demolished the entire image had they been able to do so.

The church did not want the masses to know the secret of the Four Great Principles symbolized by the Sphinx, as that knowledge would have destroyed the anthropomorphic god invented by the church. So the church fathers were careful to see that all ancient writings, which revealed the true interpretation of the symbolism of the Sphinx, were destroyed.

The essence of the teachings of the Masters is concealed from the exoteric in their symbols and allegories, which cannot be correctly interpreted unless we know something of the inner and esoteric meaning of these teachings. After the church fathers compiled their Bible for their use, they burned the ancient literature and the libraries to keep the secret meaning of these teachings from the masses.

The church fathers did not want the masses to know that they had personalized the ancient symbols and literalized the ancient allegories. The gospel Jesus is nothing more than a personalization of various cosmic principles and powers, and the gospel narratives are nothing more than the literalization of ancient allegories.

Chapter 11 — Ancient Wisdom

When the people who are known to us under the name of "ancient Egyptians" occupied the Valley of the Nile, they found, half buried in the sands, the pyramids and the Sphinx, the meaning and significance of which were quite incomprehensible to them. The Sphinx looked toward the East, so it was called the image of Harmakuti or the "Sun of the Horizon".

The Sphinx is indisputably one of the most, if not the most, remarkable of the world's works of art. It belongs to quite another art than the art we know. It appears unmistakably to be a relic of another, a very ancient, culture, which was possessed of knowledge far greater than our own.

There is a tradition that it is a great, complex hieroglyph, or book in stone, containing the whole totality of Ancient Wisdom, and reveals its message to him who can read this strange cipher which is embodied in the forms, correlations, and measurements of the different parts of the Sphinx.

This is the famous riddle of the Sphinx, which from the most ancient times many wise men have attempted to solve.

The Light of Pure Thought is too bright for man's eyes, especially when he sees it for the first time, because he has not the required preparation. There is terrible power and danger in new ideas which appear unexpectedly. The Sphinx with its riddle expressed the same idea. Legend said that it devoured those who approached it and could not solve the riddle.

The symbology of the Sphinx means that there are deep questions of the mysteries of Life which man should not approach unless he knows how to answer them, or is prepared to accept the answer when given to him.

Having once come in contact with certain ideas, man is unable to live as he lived before. He must either go farther, or parish under a burden which is too heavy for him to carry.

An inscription of the 4th dynasty, extending back 4,000 years before the dawn of the Roman State Church, mentions the Sphinx as then being a monument so old that its origin was lost in the night of time and that it had been discovered by accident, buried in the sand, beneath which it had stood forgotten for unknown ages.

Chapter 12 — Four Great Principles

Only God can grow a tree, says a theologian. But what does he mean by "God"? For that question, he has no reasonable nor satisfactory answer.

All observation and experience, covering hundreds of thousands of years, show that (1) Soil, (2) Solar Heat, (3) Air, and (4) Water produce not only the vegetable kingdom, but the animal kingdom as well.

Without these Four Great Principles, all the gods ever invented by man would be utterly useless and helpless, and there could be made nothing that is, or has been, made.

We now find a highly important secret, an ancient secret which the church buried so deeply in the 4th century that its discovery and recovery appeared impossible. In his History of Magic (1853), Eliphas Levi, great French mystic and kabbalist, described the lost and hidden message of the Sphinx as follows: "The symbolic tetrad, represented in the Ancient Mysteries by the four forms of the Sphinx-man, eagle, lion, and the bull -- corresponded with the Four Principle Elements of the Universe -- earth, water, air, and fire.

These four zodiac signs, with all their analogies, explained the one WORD hidden in all the sanctuaries (of the ancient world) . . . Moreover, the Secret WORD was never pronounced; it was always spelt, and expressed in four words, which are the sacred words "Yod-He-Vau-He" (Pike, p.763)

Chapter 13 — Je-Ho-Vah

A strange unexplained statement appears in the Bible, where the Hebrew God gave himself a new name. There it is stated: "I appeared unto Abraham, unto Isaac, and unto Jacob, by the name of God Almighty, but by the name Je-Ho-Vah was I not known to them". (Exodus 6:3)."

On its face, the statement seems to show that the Hebrews found their Je-Ho-Vah at the later time, perhaps by coming in contact with some other tribe, which had a god who seemed more attractive and powerful than their god, so they adopted him.

In Hebrew, the word Je-Ho-Vah consists of the four letters, Yod-He-Vau-He, and was termed the Tetragrammation, or four-lettered name. And it was forbidden to the Jews to pronounce it; it was also called the Ineffable Name.

All this prohibiting and forbidding seems to have been for the purpose of concealing from the masses the fact that the Ineffable Name applied not to any god, but to the Four Great Principles of Creation, symbolized by the Sphinx, in their various manifestations, which constitute the basis of the Kabbala.

The Four Letters conceal a deep symbolic meaning. The first letter, called Yod, expressed the active principle (initiative). The second letter, called He, the passive principle (receptive). The third letter, Vau, equilibrium, form, also a "like" or "bridge" that united the two, and this union produced the next creation or the second "He".

In Kaballa, the secret word Yod-He-Vau-He represented Je-Ho-Vah. Yod represented the Divine Man, and "He" represented the physical man. Vau was the "bridge" uniting the two. Kabbalists affirm that every phenomena and every object consists of these Four Principles.

A study of the Secret Name, and the finding of it in everything, constitute the chief goal of Kaballistic philosophy. Kaballists hold that these Four Cosmic Principles permeate and compose everything, and that is what the church says of its God, in these words: "By a paradox that defies the reasoning faculty, but which is readily resolved intuitively, God is apart from, and independent of, the universe; and yet he permeates every atom of it". But the church is unable to tell what he is.

By discovering these Four Principles in objects and phenomena of quite different categories, between which the man in darkness sees nothing in common, the Initiate sees the analogy between all objects and all phenomena and is convinced that all things are constructed and constituted according to the same plan.

The concept is quite clear: If the Ineffable Name (Four Cosmic Principles) is in everything, then everything should be analogous to the whole -- the atom analogous to the universe, and all analogous to the Ineffable Name. So, a study of the Law of the Four Letters, the Ineffable Name, constitutes the direct means of improving knowledge and of increasing consciousness.

The fact that all living things have a common ancestor is all that Darwin ever discovered in his great investigations and research work. And that knowledge was taught by the Ancient Masters for thousands of years before Darwin was ever born, and that is what we are showing here.

It was to suppress this knowledge that the church had the ancient literature and the ancient libraries burned.

The true meaning of the Secret WORD had to be destroyed in order to make safer the birth of the anthropomorphic God of the church.

Chapter 14 — The Secret Word

We have heard much about the Logos and the Lost Word, concerning which the Masonic Encyclopedia says: "The mythical history of Freemasonry informs us that there once existed a WORD of surpassing value and claiming a profound veneration; that this WORD was known to but few; that it was at length lost; and that a temporary substitute for it was adopted." (p.453)

Masons are still searching for that "lost WORD". If they found it, they would not know it; for they do not know what they are searching.

The "lost WORD", symbolized by the Sphinx and expressed in Four Words, was used by the Masters to indicate the Four Cosmic Principles of Creation.

That is the mysterious reason why all nations of antiquity regarded the Sphinx as an object of awe and reverence, compelling adoration and worship.

Here is where the Secret WORD was lost: When the Roman State Church was founded in the 4th century, the church fathers stole the Secret WORD, and changed its meaning, calling it God, the anthropomorphic creator.

Then they loudly proclaimed to the world that while the ancient heathens worshipped a plurality of gods, they had adopted the only true God, whom they found hiding up in the sky (John. 17:3).

Not only that, but the church fathers made their god so humanistic, so anthropopathic, that he performed functions that are performed by the human body, and begat a son, as other men do., and this son, said the church, was the "Lord and Saviour of the world".

So sayeth the Bible, which the church claims is the "word" of this God. This humanistic, anthropopathic God was invented by the church fathers and used to replace the Symbol that represented the Four Cosmic Principles of Creation (Transformation).

Note how cleverly they wove the "Word" into the John gospel -- "In the beginning was the Word, the Word was with God, and the Word was God". (John 1:1).

This is a process of metamorphosis performed by the church fathers. This "sleight-of-hand" trick of the pious fathers foisted upon the deceived masses a personalization of an ancient symbol, about which Paul (Pol. Polos, Apollo, Apollonius of Tyana) said: "In him we live and move and have our being" (Acts 17:28)

Very true -- when we know what it all means. And that is another graphic illustration which shows how craftily the church fathers inseparably connected falsehoods with undeniable truth in preparing their Bible; so intricately and delicately interweaving the true with the false, that it is absolutely impossible for the unprepared mind to separate the one from the other.

Down thru the centuries, the Catholic and Christian nations have regarded as an object of awe and reverence, compelling adoration and worship, the anthropomorphic God that was born of the Sphinx.

Now we know why it was so necessary for the church fathers to see that all ancient literature and all ancient libraries were burnt and destroyed.

Now we know why the members of the Roman Catholic Church, down to this good day, are told what they may read and what they shall not read. The purposes of the "confession box" is to see that the enslaved members obey the church orders and decrees and remain in darkness and ignorance of the facts. Now we know the deep mystery of the church God and can tell little Johnnie who made that God.

These deceived nations little suspect, when they pray to and worship their God, that they are performing obeisance unto a symbolical object of the Masters which represents the Four Cosmic Principles of Creation.

When the clergy shout that God is all and is in all, they are right; but they don't know their God, nor what their God represents. In our schools and churches, our children are solemnly taught to worship and pray to this imaginary God, believing that in so doing they are preparing a safe and serene place for their Soul when they die.

That false and deceptive practice provides a living for a principal reason why "better schools build better communities".

Chapter 15 — The Tarot

The Tarot is a pack of cards used for card-playing and fortune-telling. The origin of the Tarot is shrouded in mystery. One account says:

"A time came when Egypt, no longer able to struggle against her invaders, prepared to die honorably. Then the Egyptian servants held a great assembly to arrange how the knowledge, which until then had been confined to men judged worthy to receive it, should be saved from destruction.

"At first they thought of confiding these secrets to virtuous men secretly recruited by the Initiates themselves, who would transmit them from generation to generation. But one of the Masters, observing that virtue is a most fragile thing, and most difficult to find, at all events in a continuous line, proposed to confide the scientific traditions to vice. The latter, he said, would never fail completely, and through it we are sure of a long and durable preservation of our principles.

"This opinion evidently prevailed, and the game chose as a vice was preferred. The small plates were then engraved with the mysterious figures which taught the most important scientific secrets; and since then, the card players have transmitted this Tarot from generation to generation far better than the most virtuous men upon earth would have done." (Ouspensky, p.202)

The ancient Egyptian pack contained 78 cards and represented the most ancient books, being a synopsis of the Hermetic Sciences with their various subdivisions, embodying the Secret Doctrine of the ages, all of which constitute the one great system of the psychological study of man in his relation to the word of noumena (spiritual) and the world of pneumona (physical).

The word Tarot is pure Egyptian, Tar being way or road, and Ro standing for King or royal -- it therefore signifies the Royal Road of Life. The cards of the Tarot are symbolic; and like all symbols that are true and basic, they reveal their secret message only to those who are capable of receiving it.

The hieroglyphics in the Egyptians, the picture writing of the Mayas, and the ideographic writing of the Chinese, are forms of symbolism derived from natural objects.

Even today, parts of the figures of the Tarot can be seen in the ruins of the temples of Thebes, capital of Egypt, 2000 B.C., especially on an ancient ceiling of one of the halls of the palace of Medinet-Abou. These temples were destroyed by the Roman army after the Roman State Church was founded.

The Tarot is they Key that unlocks the mythical doctrines and philosophies of the Ancient Masters and came to be called Arcana of the Clavicles of Solomon. It is symbolized by a Key whose head is a circle containing the Four Fixed signs of the Zodiac and symbolized in the Sphinx as the Bull, the Lion, the Eagle, and the head of the Divine Man, called the Angel.

The Powers concealed in these Four Symbols are summed up by Eliphas Levi in these words: "To attain the sanctum regnum, that is the knowledge and power of the magic, there are four indispensable conditions: (1) an Intelligence illuminated by study; (2) an Intrepidity which nothing can check, (3) a Will which nothing can break, and (4) a Discretion which nothing can interrupt or intoxicate. To Know, To Dare, To WIll, and To Keep SIlent -- such are the Four Words of the Magus, inscribed upon the Four Symbolica Forms of the Sphinx". (Transcendental Magic, p.30)

From a book by Papus on the Tarot of the Bohemians, the following is condensed:

Card 1: The Juggler

I saw a strange-looking man. His figure clad in a multi-colored jester's dress stood between Earth and Sky. His feet were hidden in grass and flowers, and his head, covered by a large hat with turned-up brim, resembling the sign of eternity, disappeared in the clouds.

In one hand, he held the Magic Wand (Caduceus), the sign of many things concerning man's body and its functions, with top end pointing toward the Sun (Fire); and with the other, he was touching the Pentacle (sign of Earth), which lay before him on a traveling juggler's stall, side by side with Cup (sign of water), and Scepter (sign of air).

There flashed in my mind the realization that I saw in action the Ineffable Name, the Secret Word, the Magic Symbols, which represent (1) To Know (Cup), (2) To Dare (Scepter), (3) To Do (Magic Wand), and (4) To Keep Silent (Pentacle).

The Juggler's face was radiant and confidant. His hands flitted about swiftly as though playing with the Four Signs, and I felt that he held some mysterious threads which connected the earth with the distant luminaries.

His every movement was full of significance, and every new combination of the Four Symbols created long series of unexpected phenomena.

For whom is all this show? I asked myself. Where are the spectators? And I heard a strange Voice say: "Are spectators necessary? Look at him more closely?" I did, and I saw that he was constantly changing. Innumerable crowds seemed to pass in front of him before me, disappearing before I tell what I saw. Then I understood that he was both the Juggler and the Spectators.

And at that moment, I saw myself in him, reflected as in a mirror; and it seemed that I was looking at myself through his eyes. But another feeling told me that there was in front of me nothing but the sky and that within myself a window opened, through which my Inner Being saw unearthly sights and heard unearthly things.

Card 0: The Fool

I saw another Man. Weary and lame, he dragged himself along a dusty road, across a treeless plain, beneath the scorching rays of the sun.

Gazing stupidly sideways with a fixed eyes, with a half-smile, half-grimace frozen upon his face, he crawled along, neither seeing nor knowing wither, plunged in his own chimerical dreams, which moved eternally in the same circle.

The fool's cap and bells were on his head back and front. His clothes were torn down the back. A wild lynx with burning eyes leaped at him from behind a stone and sank its teeth into his leg. He stumbled, nearly falling, but dragged himself ever further, carrying over his shoulder a sack full of useless things, which only his madness forced him to carry.

In front the road was cleft by a ravine. A deep precipice awaited the crazy wanderer and a huge crocodile with gaping jaws crept out of the abyss. And I heard the Voice saying to me: "Behold! This is the same Man."

Everything became confused in my head. "What has he in his sack?" I asked, not knowing why I did so. After a long silence the Voice answered: "The Four Magic Symbols, the Wand, the Cup, the Sword, and the Pentacle. The fool always carried them with him, but he does not know what they mean. Do you not see that it is you, yourself?"

And with a feeling of horror, I felt that this also was I.

Card 2: High Priestess

As I lifted the first veil and entered the outer court of the Temple of Initiation, I saw in the semi-darkness the form of a Woman (Isis), sitting on a throne between two columns, one white (Positive), and one black (Negative),

Mystery emanated from her and around her. Sacred symbols gleamed on her green robe. In her right hand she held, partly opened, the Book of the Law, which was partially hidden from the profane within the folds of her Mantle. In her left hand, she held the symbol of her authority as interpreter of the Law, two crossed Keys, one positive and the other negative.

On her head was a Golden Tiara, surmounted by the lunar crescent, symbol of her feminine functions and her power as Producer of the Race. She ruled not by might nor force, but by the mysterious power of Mother-Love, which, under the influence of the invisible and periodic forces of the moon, enabled her to produce, as it also does the earth.

The two columns expressed, from this inner or feminine aspect, the same meaning as two arms of the Juggler expressed outwardly, i.e., positive and negative. On her breast, the Priestess bore the Solar Cross, the symbol that must ever express the crucifixion -- the power of Spirit to penetrate Matter; the Light to illumine darkness, and that which is inner and sacred to express outwardly in the life.

Between the two columns behind the Woman hung a second veil, all embroidered with green leaves and pomegranate fruits. The Veil symbolized the sacred Mystery of Motherhood, not to be rudely lifted by the profane nor desecrated by the impious.

(Note: Isis was represented in the Egyptian Mysteries as having Seven Veils which shroud the mystery of birth, hence birth is the most profound and most sacred of all mysteries and has its correspondence on the Seven Planes of Consciousness.)

And the Voice said to me: "To enter the temple, it is necessary to lift the second veil and pass between two columns. In order to pass, it is necessary to produce possession of the keys, to read the book, and to understand the symbols. For the Knowledge of Good and Evil awaits you. Are you ready?" (Note: In the Ancient Temples of Isis, it was death to do so much as touch the Veil before Her Shrine.)

With deep misgiving, I felt that I was afraid to enter the Temple. "Are you ready?" repeated the Voice. I was silent. My heart nearly stopped with fear. I could not utter a word. I felt that a precipice was opening before me and that I should not dare to take a single step. Then the Woman turned her face to me and looked at me without saying a word. And I understood that she was speaking to me, but my fear only grew greater; and I knew instinctively that I should not enter the Temple.

Card 21: The World

There rose before me an unexpected Vision. A circle (Zodiac) resembling a wreath woven from rainbows and lightning revolved between Sky and Earth. It whirled with terrific speed, blinding me with its brilliance; and in this radiance and fire, music sounded and soft singing was heard and also peals of thunder and the hurricane's roar, and the noise of mountain avalanches and the rumble of earthquakes.

The circle whirled with a terrible noise, touching Earth and Sky, and in its center I saw the dancing figure of a beautiful woman, wrapped in a light transparent scarf, with a magic wand in her hand (Caduceus).

At the sides of the circle there became visible to me, the four beasts of the Apocalypse -- one like a Lion, the second like a Calf, the third with the face of a man, and the fourth like a flying Eagle.

The vision disappeared as suddenly as it had come; and a strange stillness settled on the Earth.

"What does this mean?" I asked in amazement. "It is the image of the World," said the Voice. "It must be understood before you can pass through the gates of the Temple. This is the World in the Circle of Time, amid the Four Principles -- this is what you always see, but never understand. Understand that all which you see, things and phenomena, are but the hieroglyphs of higher ideas."

The student should now read 1st chapter of Ezekiel and 7th chapter of Daniel, also chapter 4 or Revelation, to the end of Revelation.

Card 3: The Empress

I felt the breath of spring; and with the fragrance of violets, lilies of the valley, the wild cherry, and the soft singing of elves was borne toward me.

Brooks murmured, green trees rustled, choirs of birds were singing, bees were droning, and everywhere was the joyful living breath of Nature. The sun shone softly, and a small white cloud hung over the woods.

In the midst of a green glade where bloomed the first yellow primroses, on a throne encircled with blossoming lilac, I saw the Empress. A green wreath adorned her golden hair. Twelve stars shone above her head. Two white wings were visible behind her back, and in one hand she held a scepter.

With a tender smile, the Empress looked about her; and beneath her glance, flowers opened and buds unfolded their green leaves. Her dress was covered with flowers, as though every flower that opened was reflected or imprinted on it and became a part of it. The sign of Virgo, the World-Mother, was carved on her marble throne.

"Oh, Queen of Life," said I, "Why is everything so radiant and happy around you? Do you not know that there are death, dark graves, cold sepulchres, cemeteries? How can you smile while looking at the unfolding flowers, when all dies and all will die, when all is condemned to death -- even that which is not yet born?"

The Empress looked at me smiling, and beneath her smile I suddenly felt that in my Soul the flower of some brighter understanding was opening, as though something was being revealed to me -- and the terror of death began to depart from me.

The student should here read verses 1 and 2 of Chapter 12 of Revelation.

Card 20: Resurrection

I saw an icy plain. A chain of mountains covered with snow shut off the horizon. A cloud rose and grew until it covered a quarter of the sky. In the midst of the cloud, there appeared two fiery wings and I saw the messenger of the Empress.

He raised his trumpet and blew a loud blast. In response the plain trembled; and with loud reverberating echoes, the mountains answered.

And one after another the graves began to open; and from them people came forth -- children, old and young, and men and women. And they stretched out their arms to the messenger of the Empress and tried to catch the sound of the trumpet.

In the sound of the trumpet I felt the smile of the Empress. And in the opening of the graves, I saw and understood the unfolding flowers. And now I understood the dark mystery of birth and death.

(Note: We do not die; we CHANGE -- in a moment, in the twinkling of an eye, at the sound of the trumpet, as stated in the Bible (1 Corinthians 15:51), and so clearly explained by Kenyon Klamonti in his book We Do Not Die.

The Emperor

After I had studied the first three numbers, it was given to me to understand the great Law of Four -- the Alpha and Omega of all. I saw the Emperor on a high throne of stone which was decorated with four ram's heads.

A golden helmet gleamed on his bow. His white beard fell over his purple mantle. In one hand he held a sphere, the symbol of his possessions; and the other, a scepter in the form of the Egyptian cross -- the sign of his power over birth. "I am the Great Law," said the Emperor. "I am the Secret Word, the Ineffable Name. The Four Letters of the Name are in me, and I am in everything.

"I am the Four Great Principles: I am in the Four Elements. I am in the Four Seasons. I am in the Four Quarters of the Earth. I am in the Four Signs of the Tarot. I am action, I am resistance, I am completion, I am result. For him who has found the way to see me, there are no mysteries on the earth.

"As the earth contains fire, water, and air, as the fourth letter of the Ineffable Name contains the first three and itself becomes the first, so my scepter contains the complete triangle and bears in itself the seed of a new triangle."

And while the Emperor spoke, his helmet and the golden armor visible beneath his mantle shone ever more fiercely, until I could no longer bear their radiance and dropped my eyes.

When I tried to raise them again, there before me was an all-pervading radiance and light and fire. And I fell prostrate worshipping the Fiery Word, the Secret Word that was hidden in all the sanctuaries of the ancient world; the Holy Word that was never pronounced; the Master Word that was in the beginning and represented the Earth and everything upon the face of the Earth and under the earth; the Word which the New

Testament says "was God," but fails to explain what "God" represents, leaving the impression that this is the same God as that -- Who talked to Adam and Eve in the Edenic Garden; Who set and ate with Abraham in his tent; Who wrestled with Jacob; Who showed Moses his back parts; Who dictated the minutest of police regulations and the dimensions of the tabernacle and its furniture; Who insisted upon and delighted in sacrifices and burnt offerings;

Who was angry, jealous, revengeful, as well as wavering and irresolute; Who allowed Moses to argue him out of his fixed resolution utterly to destroy his people; Who commanded the performance of the most shocking and hideous acts of cruelty and barbarity; Who hardened the heart of Pharaoh; Who repented of the evil that he had said he would do unto the people of Nineveh, and who did it not, to the disgust and anger of Jonah.

Card 19: The Sun

After this, when I first saw the Sun, I understood that it is itself the expression of the Fiery Word and the sign of the Emperor.

The Great Luminary shone and gave warmth and Life. Below, tall golden sunflowers nodded their heads. And I saw two children in a garden behind a high enclosure. The Sun poured its warm rays on them, and to me it seemed that the golden rain was falling upon them; as though the Sun shed molten gold over the Earth.

For an instant I closed my eyes. When I opened them again, I saw that every ray of the Sun was the scepter of the Emperor, which bore within it universal Life!

And I saw how, beneath the sharp points of the Sun's rays, the mystical flowers of the waters were unfolding everywhere and how the rays penetrated into the flowers; and how all of Nature was continually born of the mysterious union of the Two Cosmic Principles, the Positive and the Negative, the Initiative and the Receptive, the Active and the Passive, the Male and the Female.

(Note: The Sun was the God of the Ancient Masters, as we have shown in our great work, Ancient Sun God. The Bible says' "For our God is a Consuming Fire," (Hebrews 12:19)

The Ancient Masters says, "The Sun of the Universe is the Saviour of the World." In their Bible, the church fathers made that read, "The Son of God is the Saviour of the World."

Card 5: The Hierophant

I saw the great Master of the Temple. He sat on a golden throne, resting upon a purple dias. He wore the robes of a High Priest and a Golden Tiara. Under his feet were two crossed Keys (positive and negative), and before him, two Initiates were bowed down. And he spoke to them.

I heard the sound of his voice but could not understand a word he said. Either he spoke in a language unknown to me, or there was something that prevented me from understanding the meaning of his words.

And the Voice said to me: "He speaks only for those who have ears to hear. But woe unto them who believe that they hear before they have heard, or hear that which he does not say, or put their own words in place of his. They will never receive the Keys of Understanding. And it is of them that it was said, "They neither go in themselves, neither are entering to go in." (Matthew 23:13)

Card 7: The Chariot

I saw a chariot drawn by two Sphinxes, a white and a black. Four pillars supported a blue canopy, spangled with five-pointed stars. Beneath the canopy, driving the sphinxes, stood the Conqueror, in armor of steel. In his hand was a scepter, surmounted with a sphere, a triangle, and a square. (Revelations 23:13).

"Everything in this picture has a meaning. Look and try to understand," said the Voice to me. "This is the Conqueror who has not yet conquered himself. Here are both Will and Knowledge . . . but in all this, there is more of the Desire to attain than Real attainment.

"The man in the chariot began to consider himself Conqueror before he actually conquered. He decided that conquest must come to a conqueror. In this there are many possibilities, but also many deceiving lights, and great dangers await the man in the chariot.

"He drives the chariot by the power of his Will and the magic sword, but the tension of his Will may weaken and the Sphinxes may pull in different directions and tear him and his chariot asunder. This is the Conqueror against whom the conquered may still rise. Do you see behind him the towers of the conquered city? Perhaps there already burns the flame of revolt."

(Note: The effects of harmful living constantly burn in the body, gently at first but ever growing more powerful as the years pass; and the body suffers till death ends the misery, which is only increased and never lessened by doctors. For the evil effects of harmful living cannot be remedied by the treatment and dope of doctors.)

"Neither does he know that within himself lies the conquered city (Revelations 21:14); that within himself the Sphinxes are watching his every movement, and that within himself great dangers await him. And realize that this is the same Man whom you saw connecting heaven and Earth, and the same Man whom you saw dragging himself along a dusty road toward the precipice where the dragon awaited him."

Card 16: The Tower

From the Earth I saw rising a high tower, whose top reached beyond the clouds. Black night was all around, and thunder rumbled. Suddenly the clouds opened; a thunderclap shook the Earth; and lightning struck the Tower.

Flames shot out of the Sky; the whole tower filled with fire and smoke; and I saw the builders of the tower falling from its top.

"Look," said the Voice, "Creation's laws hate deceit, and man cannot subjugate himself to its laws. Creation is patient for a long time, and then suddenly, with one blow, it annihilates all that violate the law. If men could only realize that almost all they know consists of the ruins of destroyed towers, perhaps they would cease to build them."

(Note: An excellent lesson; but few ever learn it. The world of science is striving to improve on Nature, while medical art constantly endeavors to make a disease-proof man, keeping the masses in ignorance of the fact that there is no disease per se. There is Good Health and Bad Health, but no disease. The symptoms of Bad Health the doctors are trained to study, group together, and give them names that mean nothing (diagnosis), and term them diseases that will kill the patient if not treated and "cured".)

Card 8: Truth

When I had secured the keys, had read the book, and understood the symbols, I was then permitted to lift the veil of the temple and enter the inner sanctuary.

There I saw a woman with a golden crown and purple mantle. In one hand she held a sword, and in the other a pair of scales. Seeing her, I trembled with fear, as her look was deep and terrible, and drew me like an abyss. "You are seeing Truth," said the Voice. "Everything is weighed in these scales. That sword is eternally lifted in defense of justice, and nothing can escape it." (This refers to Cosmic Law).

"But why do you turn your eyes from the scales and sword? Are you afraid? Yes you are, as they deprived you of your last illusion. How will you live on Earth without these illusions? You wanted to see Truth, and now you see Her.

"Remember what awaits man when he has seen the goddess. He will never again be able to close his eyes to what does not please him, as he has done hitherto. He will see Truth perpetually and in everything. Can you bear this? Having seen Truth, you now have to go further, even though you do not wish to do so."

Card 15: Evil

Black night enveloped the Earth, and in the distance burned a red flame. A strange fantastic figure grew visible to me as I drew nearer. High Above the Earth I saw the hideous red face of Evil, sitting on a black cube, in front of which a man and a woman were chained to an iron ring. They were the same man and woman I had seen in the garden.

"These are the same people," said the Voice,"but they began to believe in themselves and in their own powers. They believed they knew what was good and evil, and mistook their weakness for strength, and then Evil subjugated them."

And I heard the voice of Evil. "I am Evil, in so far as evil can exist in this world. In order to perceive me, one must see crookedly, wrongly, and narrowly. Three paths lead to me: conceit, suspicion, and accusation. My chief virtues are calumny and slander. I complete the triangle, the other sides being Death and Time.

"In order to escape from this triangle, it is only necessary to see that it does not exist. But how to do that is not for me to tell. For I am Evil, which men invented in order to hold me responsible for all the errors and wrongdoing of which they themselves are guilty."

Card 14: Time

I saw an Angel standing between Earth and Heaven clothed in white, with wings of flame and a golden halo round his head. He stood with one foot on the land and the other on the sea, and behind him the Sun was rising.

On the Angel's breast was the sign of the Sacred Book of the Tarot -- the square, and within it the triangle. On his brow was the sign of eternity and life -- the Circle. In one hand, he held a cup of gold and a cup of silver in the other. Between the cups there flowed an incessant stream but I could not tell from which cup it flowed and into which it was flowing. With terror I understood that I had to come to the last of the mysteries, from which there is no return.

"The name of the Angel is Time," said the Voice. "On his forehead is the circle, the sign of Eternity and the sign of Life.

In the Angel's hand are two cups. One cup is the past, the other the future. The stream between them is the present. You can see that it is flowing in both directions. This is Time in its most incomprehensible aspect for man.

"Men think that everything is incessantly flowing in one direction. They do not see that everything eternally meets, that one thing comes from the past and another from the future, and that Time is a multitude of circles turning in different directions."

Card 10: Wheel of Fortune

I was absorbed in deep meditation, trying to understand my vision of the Angel. Raising my head suddenly, I saw in the midst of the sky an immense revolving circle covered with Kaballistics letters and signs. The circle revolved with great speed; and together with it now rising, now falling, revolved the symbolic figures of the serpent and the ram; and on the top of the circle sat the Sphinx.

At the four quarters of the sky I saw on the clouds the four winged beasts of the Apocalypse -- one like a lion, another like a calf, the third with the face of a man, and the fourth like a flying eagle -- and each was reading an open book.

And I heard the voice of the animals of Zarathustra: "Everything goes, everything returns; eternally rolls the wheel of being. Everything dies, everything is born again; eternally runs the year of being. Being begins in every Now, around every "Here" rolls the sphere of "there". The middle is everywhere. Crooked is the path of eternity.

Card 13: Death

Wearied by the speed of the Wheel of Fortune, I sank to the ground and closed my eyes. But to me the wheel was still revolving, and the four beasts on the clouds still sat and read their books. Suddenly, opening my eyes, I saw a horseman on a white charger, clad in black armor with a black helmet and a black plume.

The face of a skeleton looked out from under the helmet. One bony hand held a black banner, gentling waving, and the other held black reins, ornamented with a skull and crossbones. Wherever the white steed passed, night and death followed, flowers withered, leaves fell, the Earth was covered with a white shroud, graveyards appeared, towers, palaces and cities fell in ruins.

Kings in the full splendor of their glory and power, beautiful women, high priests, innocent children -- all, at the approach of the white steed, fell on their knees in terror and stretched out their hands in anguish. In the distance behind the towers, the sun was setting.

The chill of death gripped me. It seemed that already I felt the hoofs of the sted on my breast, and I saw the whole world falling into an abyss.

Suddenly I felt something familiar in the measured step of the horse, something I had heard and seen before. Another instant, and I head in its step the movement of the Wheel of Fortune.

Light broke in upon me, and gazing at the disappearing horseman and the setting sun, I understood that the Path of Life consists of the hoof-marks of the Steed of Death (Revelations 6:8).

The sun, setting on one side, rises on the other. Every moment of its motion is a setting at one point and a rising at another. And I understood that just as the sun rises in its setting and sets in its rising, so Life dies when it is born, and is born again when it dies (John. 3:3, 5, 7).

"Yes," said the Voice,"You think the sun has only one aim, to set and to rise. The Sun goes on it way, over its own orbit, round an unknown Center. Life, Death, Sunrise, and Sunset -- are you not aware that all these are but thoughts, illusions, dreams, and fears of the Fool?"

Card 12: The Hanged Man

And I saw a man with his hands tied behind his back, hanging by one leg from high gallows with head downward, and in fearful torments. Round his head was a golden halo.

And I heard a Voice, which said to me: "Behind, this is the man who has seen Truth.

"New suffering, such as no earthly misfortune can ever cause, that is what awaits man on earth when he finds the path to Eternity and the understanding of the Infinite. He is still man, but he already knows many things inaccessible even to the gods. And this conflict between the large and the little in his soul makes his torture and his Golgotha.

"In his own Soul is raised a high gallows on which he hangs in suffering, feeling as though he were turned head downward. He chose his way. It is for this that he went a long journey from trial to trial, from initiation to initiation, through failures and through falls. And now he has found Truth and knows himself.

"He now knows that it is he who stands between Earth and Heaven, controlling the elements with the magical symbols; and it is also he who walks in the Fool's cap along a dusty road, beneath the blazing sun, toward the abyss where the dragon awaits him.

"It is he with the woman in the Garden of Eden, under the protection of the beneficent Genie. It is also he who is bound with the woman in the black cube of lies. It is he who stands as the Conqueror for a moment in the deceptive chariot, drawn by the Sphinxes, ready to rush in opposite directions; and it is he again in the desert who looks for Truth with a lantern in the bright light of day. And now he has found Truth."

(Note: The body, with arms extended and feet together, is a symbol of the cross on which man hangs for evil purposes. He uses his body to satisfy his lusts for sensation, greed, hate, jealousy, etc.)

Chapter 16 — Psychology and Metaphysics

Like other ancient writings, the Hebrew alphabet is completely symbolic. The letters of this alphabet and the various allegories of the Kabbala; the names of metals, acids, and salts in alchemy; the names of planets and constellations in astrology; the names of good and evil spirits in magic -- all these were nothing more than a conventional hidden language for psychological and metaphysical concepts.

The open study of these subjects, especially in their wider sense, was impossible in the dark ages. Torture and the iron stake awaited the investigators then and would now if the Roman Catholic Church were all-powerful as it was then. As we gaze deeper into the dark ages, we see still more fear of all attempts to study man.

Amidst all the darkness, ignorance, and superstition created by the church, it was impossible to speak and act openly. Those who tried it were burned at the stake. The open study of psychology is under suspicion even now, which is considered a time of enlightenment.

The true essence of the Hermetic Science was a secret and was hidden in the symbols of Alchemy, Astrology, Magic, and the Kabbala. Alchemy assumed the ostensible aim in the preparation of gold, of the discovery of the elixir of life. Astrology and the Kabbalah, divination; and Magic, the subjugation of spirits.

When the true alchemist spoke of the search for gold, the disciplines knew he referred to the search for gold in the soul of man. When he spoke of the elixir of life, he referred to the search for eternal life. In these cases, he called "gold" what in the New Testament is termed the Kingdom of Heaven.

When the true astrologer spoke of planets and constellations, he referred to the planets and constellations in the soul of men, i.e., of the properties of the soul and its relation to the physical and spiritual worlds.

When the true Kabbalist spoke of the Ineffable Name, he had in mind the Four Cosmic Principles of the Universe and not the things said in dead books nor in the Biblical text.

When the true Magician spoke of the subjugation of "spirits", elements, and the like in the will of man, he meant the subjugation to one single will of the different "I's" of men, his different desires and tendencies. Alchemy, Astrology, Magic, and the Kabbalah are parallel symbolical systems of psychology and metaphysics.

Chapter 17 — Initiation

Initiation into the Ancient Mysteries was conducted by the means of a mystic drama, representing the progress of man, from the ignorance of darkness to the Light of Truth. The ceremony of initiation itself was a progress through gloom and terror and all possible mortal horrors, to scenes of indescribable beauty and glory.

The chief center of the Egyptian Mysteries was at Memphis. They were of two degree -- the Lesser and the Greater. The latter was taught by the Masters of Osiris and Serapis; and the former by those of Isis. The candidate was required to furnish proofs of a pure and moral life as evidence that he was fitted for admission or enrollment.

When these conditions were fulfilled, he was required to spend a week in solitude and meditation, abstain from all unchaste acts, confine himself to a frugal diet, and to purify the body by frequent ablutions.

Being thus prepared, the candidate was ordered to enter the Pyramid during the night, where he had to descend on hands and knees through a narrow passage without steps, until he reached a cave-like opening; thru which he had to crawl to another subterranean cave, on the walls of which were inscribed the following words:

"The mortal who shall travel over this road alone, without hesitating or looking back, shall be purified by Fire, by Water, and by Air, and if he can surmount the fear of death, he shall emerge from the bosom of the Earth; he shall revisit the Light, and claim the right of preparing his Soul for the reception of the mysteries of the Great Goddess Isis.

At the same time three men, disguised in masks and resembling the heads of jackals, and armed with swords, sought to frighten him, first by their appearance and noise, and afterward by enumerating the dangers that waited him on his journey.

If his courage did not fail here, he was permitted to pass on to the Hall of Fire. This was a large apartment lined with burning stuffs, and the Floor was a great painted flame color. The bars of the grate were so narrow that they offered scarcely space enough for him to cross. Through this hall he was obliged to pass quickly to avoid the effects of the flames and heat.

He next encountered a wide channel fed from the waters of the Nile River. Over this stream he had to swim, with a small lamp which furnished all the light that was afforded him. On reaching the opposite side, he found a narrow passage leading to a landing place about six feet square, with a movable floor. On each side were walls of stone; and behind wheels of metal were fixed. In front was an ivory gate, opening inward, and preventing any further advance.

On attempting to turn two large rings annexed to the door, in hopes of continuing his journey, the wheels came into motion, producing a most terrific effect; and the floor gave way, leaving him suspended by the arms over apparently a deep abyss, from which came a violent current of cold air, so that the lamp was extinguished, and he was in complete darkness.

In this process of trial, the candidate was exposed to the action of the Four Great Purifying Elements -- Earth, Fire, Water, and AIr.

After the risk of falling into an unknown depth had continued for a moment, the floor resumed its original position, the wheels stopped, and the ivory door flew open, disclosing the sanctuary of Isis, illuminated with a blaze of light, where the priests of that Goddess were assembled, in two ranks, clothed in ceremonial dress, and hearing the mysterious symbols of the Order, singing hymns in praise of their divinity, who welcomed and congratulated the candidate on his courage and escape from the dangers which had surrounded him.

The entrance to the sanctuary was constructed in the pedestal of the triple statue of Osiris, Isis, and Horus; and the walls were ornamented with various allegorical figures, symbols of the Egyptian Mysteries, among which were particularly prominent: (1) A serpent casting an egg out of its mouth, A symbol of all things by the heat of the sun (not by the Christian God). (2) A serpent coiled in the form of a Circle, holding its tail in its mouth; a symbol of eternity, and of the constant revolution of the Sun. (3) The double Tau, a symbol of the Active and Passive Power of Cosmic Processes in the production of all things.

There the candidate was ordered to kneel before an altar and required to pronounce the following obligation: "I do most solemnly swear of my own free will and accord that I shall never reveal to any uninitiated person the things I have seen in this sanctuary, nor any of the mysteries which have been or shall be communicated to me. I call on all the deities of the earth, of the sky, and of the infernal regions, to be witnesses of this oath; and I trust that their vengeance will fall on my head should I ever become a villain so based and perjured."

The candidate was then retained for several months in the temple, where moral trials of different kinds awaited him, the object of which was to bring out all the traits of his character.

After he had passed thru this trial, then came what was called his Manifestation. This consisted of a number of ceremonies, of which the voice was the subject for twelve days.

He was dedicated to Osiris, Isis, and Horus, and decorated with the twelve consecrated scarfs and the Olympic cloak.

These scarves were embroidered with the twelve signs if the Zodiac and the cloak with figures that were symbolic of the starry sky. A crown of palm leaves was placed upon his head and a burning torch in his hand. Thus prepared, he was again led to the altar and required to renew his oath.

This, the first degree as we may term it, was initiation into the mysteries of Isis. All the details of it were never known except to the Initiates themselves. Isis, says Knight, was the personification of universal nature. To the candidate she said, “I am nature, the parent of all things, the sovereign of the elements, the primary progeny of time.”

Plutarch tells us that on the front of the temple of Isis was placed this inscription: “I, Isis, am all that has been, that is, or shall be; and no mortal hath ever unveiled me.” Thus we may conjure that the Isiac mysteries were descriptive of the alternate decaying and renovating if the things of nature.

Higgins says that in the mysteries of Isis were dramatized the misfortunes and tragic death of Isiris (who symbolized mankind) and his resurrection to Eternal Life. Into the Egyptian Mysteries were initiated Herodotus, Plutarch, Pythagoras, and Apollonius; and Herodotus and Plutarch have given brief accounts of them.

But their own knowledge must have been extremely limited, for Clement of Alexandria said that the more important secrets of Life were not revealed to even to all the priests, but only to a select number of them.

These Mysteries exercised a powerful influence over the Egyptian people. They gave unity to the Egyptian character, consistency to their religious establishments, and vigor and directness in the pursuits of philosophy, science, and art.

The world has not been told that the great Greek philosophers got their education in the Egyptian Mysteries and that Pythagoras spent twenty years there in study under the Egyptian Masters.

The Egyptian Mysteries were destroyed by the Roman army when Constantine founded the Roman Catholic Church in the 4th century. When this man had reached the peak of his mighty power, like most other men, he wanted to be still greater. He craved more power. He was motivated by the vain ambition to have the exclusive religious power of the world as well as the political power.

He would go to the very center of the great religion which ruled the subjects of his fast realm, import to Rome its most precious principles and precepts, then revise these to serve his purposes, invent a popular name for his new religion, and then conceal his fraudulent work by sending his army to demolish the ancient temples of Egyptian Libraries.

To make his work the more secure, effective, and complete, he would murder the masters of the old religion and then discredit and disgrace their country by stigmatizing it, "Land of Darkness".

Why should Egypt, the Land of Light and Learning, suddenly sink so low as to be termed the "Land of Darkness"? Concerning this, one able scholar wrote: "Why Egypt, was called the 'Land of Darkness' is difficult to understand. There are many lands on earth today which at one time rose to great heights in cultural and intellectual development and then sank to very low level; but none of these is commonly referred to as the 'Land of Darkness' -- symbolic prophecy of the Great Pyramid."

When the facts are known, the answer to that question is easy to find. Livingston has that answer in his Book of David under the subhead, "The Constantine Bible". (p.140)

He did not term it the Christian Bible, nor the Roman Catholic Bible. He knew who established Roman Catholicism and who directed the work by compiling the writings that appear in the so-called "Holy Bible". How carefully and how well have the Roman Catholic historians concealed the actual facts of ancient history,

Chapter 18 — Four Fixed Signs

The church fathers were careful to hide the fact that the Sphinx, the Four Fixed Signs of the Zodiac, and the Great Pyramid, symbolize the Four Cosmic Elements which constitute man, as follows: 1. Solar Radiation is the Spark of Life; 2. Air is the Breath of Life; 3. Water is the River of Life; 4. Dust of the Earth is the Body of Life.

In the New Testament the Four Fixed Signs are represented by the four gospels. That is the secret reason why only four were included in the Bible, of the many gospels then in circulation, as related in the first line of Luke.

1. Matthew, "the Man from the East" (Aquarius--waterman) is the adjuster of conditions produced by man's ignorance. He is called the Publican or Tax-gatherer, the one who levies upon mankind the tribute to knowledge.

2. Mark is the Lion (Leo), the power to Dare. He adjusts the conditions which arise from the lack, perversion, or fickleness of love, which should be the Foundation Stone of the spiritual life, the rock of Intuition.

3. Luke, the Bull (Taurus), is called the Physician. As the Bull symbolizes the masses who toil and labor, Luke adjusts the conditions produced by the improper use or enslavement of labor. This he accomplishes through the power of attainment through patient perseverance, the power to DO.

4. John, the Eagle (Scorpio, the power to Keep Silent), adjusts the ills resulting from the stinging power of the Scorpion (carnal lust) by lifting up the Mind to dwell in the higher realms symbolized by the eagle's wings, the fowl of the air.

Chapter 19 — Angelic Plan

The Human Head, rising above the body of the Sphinx, symbolized the ancient doctrine of the Divine Man, exalted high above propensities and passions of his animalistic nature. He was as free of carnal lust "as the angels in heaven". (Mark 12:25)

This doctrine is symbolized in the Bible as the mysterious "war in heaven" (Revelations 12:7), which we interpret in detail in the Great Red Dragon. "Heaven" is not a place in space but the Divine Mind in the kingdom within (Luke 17:21). "For the kingdom of heaven is not meat and drink, but righteousness and peace" (of Mind) (Romans 14:17).

As we show in another work, the Great Red Dragon and his divinities symbolize man's animalistic nature (Revelations 12:9) -- From the sky (Mind), they are cast down by Michael and his hosts, which symbolize man's Purity of thoughts.

To the esoteric, this symbology means that the Mind has been purged and purified of the taint of Carnality. "For to be carnally minded is death." (Romans 8:6).

The masters consistently taught, and it runs thru the Bible like a stream of fire, that man must conquer and control his body, and must subdue his Animal Nature before he can gain freedom from its Power and enjoy the higher consciousness that results from a activation of the Seven Seals -- the Seven major nerve ganglia of his body, as described by Klamonti in his great work titled, Awaken The World Within. Otherwise, the Animalistic Plane is the only realm of which he can have conscious knowledge, and the Angelic Plane will be unknown to him.

The best literature on this subject comes from India, where the ancient philosophers preached, as with a voice of thunder, to subdue the passions of the five senses. They termed 'lust" and temptation the sharks and dragons in the river of life, and that is mentioned in the Bible. (Isaiah 27:1, Ezekiel 29:3) They said that "he who rejoices in the pleasure of the senses and passions is like a thirsty man drinking poison to quench his thirst."

The essence of the New Testament is not a Savior who died on the cross, but the negation of sex and the recommendation of genuine and pure celibacy is expressed in such sayings as "concerning virgins, , , it is good for a man so to be; it is good for a man not to touch a woman." It is even stated that it is good not to marry (Matthew 19:10; 1 Corinthians 7:1, 25, 26).

But "all men cannot receive this saying" (Matthew 19:11), since it is intended for those only who seek to rise to the angelic plane; and few there be in that class. The natural (physical, animal) man received not the things of the spirit. . .they are foolishness to him; only he that is ready to receive it will receive it. (Matthew 19:12; 1 Corinthians 2:14).

Mere animalistic sex expression has no more place in a highly cultured civilization than would mud-huts serve as modern homes. But in our pseudo-civilization, worse than animalistic sex misuses are indulged in and condoned.

The greatest work on the subject produced in modern times was written by Dr. G.R. Clements in 1931, being a course of 85 lessons titled, Science of Regeneration, in which he presented overwhelming evidence to show that in the beginning, propagation was the result of parthenogenesis.

The press of June 30, 1956, said: "A sensational claim in England that a woman there had a child in a virgin birth was greeted with skepticism today by American gynecologists and other experts. According to the British report, published by the mass circulation London Sunday Pictorial in a copyrighted story, a research team of doctors had examined the woman and her child -- a girl now 11 years old -- for six months.

"The medical findings, according to the story, were that the doctors could find no evidence to disprove the woman's claim that the child was born "entirely without a man'. It was claimed that the birth was the result of parthenogenesis -- reproduction without fertilization from a male."

The fact that the child was a girl is more evidence to support the claim, as it is said that in the cause of parthenogenesis, the progeny is always female.

Chapter 20 — The Great Pyramid

The Great Pyramid of Gizeh was one of the chief temples of the Ancient Mysteries.

The giant structure of stone, built thousands of years ago by scientists with a knowledge of astronomy and mathematics so high, and with the use of instruments of such remarkable precision, that modern scientists stand before it in awe. All the other pyramids in Egypt are but copies of this one.

The giant edifice, declared Prof, Thevenin, reveals amazing knowledge of a race of Supermen who lived on earth more than fifty thousand years ago and is said to be the oldest building on the face of the earth.

Pyra is Greek for Fire, or Light, or the Illumination that reveals something or makes things visible in darkness, as well as giving heat. Midos is Greek and means "measures".

The words Pyra and Midos the Greeks adopted from the Phoenician word "Purimmiddah". The form of the Pyramid represents the ascending Flame, flying upward toward its origin -- a symbol of the Spark of Eternal Life -- returning to the Sun of the Universe.

Fire is the most ancient symbol of Life, and the Sun was regarded as its source, as we have shown in our work titled, Eternal Life. For that reason, the ancient Egyptians ascribed divinity to the Sun.

But long ages before the Egyptians, the primeval race of Aryans worshipped the solar Orb in its various manifestations as the Generator of Light and Life.

In the Vedic hymns appear perpetual allusions to the sun with its life-bestowing rays. The 97th Psalm is a lyric to the Sun.

The Persians, Assyrians, and Chaldeans all worshipped the Sun as the Generator of Light and Life. Sun-worship is the oldest and by far the most prevalent of all ancient religions and is frequently mentioned in the Bible. (Ezekiel 8:16)

Holy Bible means Sun Book. Helics is Greek for Sun, and Biblia is Greek for book. So the Bible was compiled from the literature of the ancient Sun Worshippers.

Chapter 21 — Four Departments of the Body

The four sides of the Pyramid, laid flat, form four triangles around the base. The four-sided base of the Pyramid represents the Four Cosmic Principles of which man's four bodies are composed. These are hydrogen, nitrogen, oxygen, and carbon -- or earth, water, air, and fire.

These principles are termed the basis of all things, and upon this base the four bodies of man are raised, each from its own elements. Thus, the dense physical body from the earth element, the fluidal body from water, the mental (aerial) body from the air, and the vital body from Fire.

The physical body is interpenetrated by a body of finer substance, vibrant at a higher rate, in which the emotions and passions register, called the fluidal body. These two bodies are interpenetrated by a third of a still finer substance, vibrating as a still higher rate, in which thoughts register, called the aerial (mental) body.

Engendering, sustaining, and informing these three bodies is the electrical (fire) body, which interpenetrates all substance, causing different rates of vibration in the different densities.

The fourth body (solar electricity) makes man a living being; and when any obstruction hinders its free, natural operation, the whole body begins to deteriorate, with complete dissolution (somatic death) and the end result, provided the obstruction is not removed in time.

This is the field of the doctors. In its efforts to remove the dangerous obstruction, the body shows symptoms of that internal struggle, which the dumb doctors erroneously term "disease", and are taught by their schools to "cure" the "disease" by suppressing the symptoms of the internal struggle.

If this dangerous work of suppression succeeds complete, the Victim dies.

Chapter 22 — The Twelve Zodiac Signs

The twelve lines used in drawing the four triangles of the four sides of the Pyramid when laid flat around the base, represent the twelvefold constitution of man as follows: 1. The Fire Triplicity, composed of Aries, Leo, and Sagittarius. These signs correspond primarily with the Spark of Life, or Electrical Body. 2. The Air Triplicity, composed of Gemini, Libra, and Aquarius. These signs correspond to the aerial or mental body. 3. The Water Triplicity, composed of Cancer, Scorpio, and Pisces. These signs correspond to the fluidal body. 4. The Earth Triplicity, composed of Taurus, Virgo, and Capricorn. These signs correspond to the earth or physical body.

The Zodiac picture of the garment of flesh worn by Spiritual Man during his earthly peregrinations. The Zodiac is the law which determines the color of the astral vibrations, the note, or number, of the Soul.

Astrology teaches that at the moment of birth, man's body corresponds in color, number, and vibration to the Solar System at that moment. He is clothed in the Zodiac.

Chapter 23 — Cosmic Chemistry

Man contains within himself all the powers, systems, planets, and globes of the universe. He is the Microcosm of the Macrosom.

The chemical elements of the universe in man's body are eternal and never change. They enter into the composition of matter, forming bodies by the process of condensation, thus making visible objects appear that are composed of invisible elements. The invisible becomes visible. Invisible gases condense and become water.

So the Masters said: "The invisible things of the universe from the creation of the world are clearly seen (in the mind), being understood by the things that are made." (visible) (Romans 1:20).

These "ancient heathens", as science calls them, knew that the air is not so void and empty as modern science thought it was.

The universe is globed in a dew-drop. A droplet of water forms a tiny microcosm containing, in a state of extreme dilution, a great variety of chemical elements, the same as those contained in man's body.

The chemical elements of all bodies, from star above to man below, are the same. They never change, never lose their identity. They enter into the composition of all things and are always governed by the same cosmic law.

Furthermore, the elements retain their true identity while in man's body, where they serve their purpose as they do in all bodies, from the invisible atom in the body cell to the giant star up in the sky.

The Masters taught that the human body is definitely related to and linked with the entire universe and all its parts and that all are ruled by the same law. The Four Cosmic Elements listed above are the builders, sustainers, and regenerators of the human body.

Chapter 24 — The Guard

The Sphinx was the Guard of the Passage leading to the Great Pyramid. The entrance was thru a secret subterranean tunnel between the Sphinx's paws. Knowledge of this tunnel was lost for ages when the blowing sand buried the Sphinx.

It was not until about 825 A.D., writes Seiss, that "one of the Mohammedan caliphs", after driving thru "full one hundred feet of rock . . . brooke into the regular passageway" (p.23)..

The huge paws of the Sphinx rest on a high wall, forming two sides of a court in front of it. In the center, between the paws, there stood in ancient days an altar, back of which and beneath the breast of the Sphinx, was the secret door to the underground passage, well guarded, and opening by the application of a secret device, known only to a few select persons.

Thru this secret door the neophyte entered the passage under the Sphinx, under the sands and foundation of the Pyramid, and extending to the reception chamber, far below the ground-level of the Pyramid.

Chapter 25 — Animal Sacrifice

As we subdue or sacrifice our animalistic nature, we rise to the angelic level.

At the shrine of the Sphinx, standing guard before the Pyramid, the pious neophyte, in his faithful search for the higher life, was halted by his guide. Then the Sphinx, thru the voice of its human guard, spoke to the neophyte in solemn tones, and this is what it said: "O man of darkness, I represent your body. If you would pass on to the Temple in your search for light, you must first master me, for I am your Animal Nature."

Again the Sphinx symbolizes the Microsom, with the Mind and Spirit of the human rising up out of the animal desires and passions. It is the riddle of the ages, and man is the answer.

Here the candidate for initiation in the Mysteries of Life was required to "sacrifice" forever his Animal Nature, in order to be permitted to pass between the paws of the Sphinx and enters the tunnel leading to the Pyramid Temple, where he was taught the mysterious lessons which would change his whole life.

This is the esoteric interpretations of that "animal sacrifice" so often mentioned in the Bible.

Moses said to Aaron, Go unto the altar, and offer thy sin offering and thy burnt offering, and make an atonement for thyself (Leviticus 9:7)

When Solomon's Temple was finished, he offered bulls (Taurus) as a sacrifice by burning them upon the temple altar (1Kings. 9:23). This "burning" symbolizes the work of the Sun. In honor of the burning orb, a light burns constantly before the Ark in the synagogue. There is a light over the Altar of the church. A light illuminates the Crescent of the Mosque. There was a light upon the hearth in ancient days. These are some of the countless signs of Sun-worship. Holy Bible means Helic Bible, or Book of the Sun-worshippers.

When Ram or Bull of the Celestial Zodiac was offered upon the altar, it symbolized the subjugation of man's animalistic nature.

In this symbolism, we visualize the trembling neophyte, symbolized in Revelation as a Lamb (5:6), passing thru his ordeals, tests, and purifications in the solemn drama of the Ancient Mysteries and offering upon the Altar of Righteousness the animalistic propensities and passions of his own nature.

Before the Solar Fire of his own body, the neophyte, advancing to the Angelic Life, makes his solemn vows; and upon the Altar of his own Spiritual Being, he lays his crown and scepter, his robes and jewels, his hates and fears, his desires and lust, sanctifying his life as "a Priest forever after the Order of Melchizedek". (the Sun God)

Paul revealed the mystic character of this Order when he said: "Without father, without mother, without descent, having neither beginning of days, nor end of life" (Hebrews 7:3). This describes the nature of the Sun. Paul also said, "Our God is a Consuming Fire". (Hebrews 12:29).

Having conquered his own body, the neophyte was no longer the lost son of the Sun, wallowing in the mire of the animalistic Plane. He was the resurrected regenerated, redeemed Son, in whom I am well pleased", and "In whom my soul delighteth: I have put my Spirit on him" (Isaiah 42:1; Matthew 3:17). The Voice of the Sun speaking to Man.

Therefore, he that conquers his animalistic nature and controls his own body shall inherit all things (good in life): and I (perfection) will be his guide, and he shall follow me in happiness (Revelations 21:7).

The allegory of man's sacrificing, upon the Altar of Righteousness in the Temple, the Animalistic Passions of his own body, was purposely related in the Bible by the church fathers in such a way as to deceive the masses. "I doubt," wrote Col. James Churchward, "whether there is a Hebrew today who knows the true meaning of the burnt sacrifice, and what it symbolized." (Lost Continent of Mu, p.309).

Chapter 26 — The Consuming Fire

The Tree in the midst of the Garden (Genesis 2:17), the Burning Bush (Exodus 3:1-4), the Fiery Serpent of Moses (Numbers 21:8), and the Red Dragon (Revelations 12) are all directly related symbology.

As we explain in much more detail in The Magic Wand, the Masters taught that at the base of the spine is in the center of the Fire of Life, the creative Fire of the Microcosm, the Fire that burns but does not consume -- immediately. That Fire consumes slowly, by inches and degrees, and commences its destruction work when the child begins to masturbate. That is the Red Dragon that stands ever ready to devour the child as soon as born (Revelations 12:4).

The press of October 27, 1955, contained the picture of a young woman in South America, age 21, with her son of 16, born when she was only five. No wonder the race degenerates and that the Masters centered their teachings on the evils of carnal lust. That is the actual battle of Armageddon that runs thru all the biblical fables and allegories.

The angel of the Lord appeared unto Moses in a flame of fire, out of the midst of a bush; and the bush burned with fire, but was not consumed (Exodus 3:1-4). Moses represents humanity, and the angel represents the Ego, the consciousness, the Real Man.

The Masters taught that by the subjugation of his animalistic nature, man not only improves every part of his body, but rises to the angelic plane by virtue of his State of Consciousness expanding and rising from the physical to the astral plane.

The Tree in the midst of the Garden represents man's Spinal Cord, whose Living Sap is a dynamic creative force, a Fire that burns but consumes not. Yes, it does consume, but so slowly and gradually that the end results are not connected with the real cause.

Its lower aspect of animalistic propagation is expressed thru the genitals, and its higher aspect of Angelic Redemption is expressed thru mysterious Pineal Gland of the Brain, the All Seeing Eye, the SIngle Eye that fills the Mind with Spirited Light (Matthew 6:22), a gland about the function of which modern science knows nothing.

Far from complete would Man be without the cosmic power of creativeness. This power presents the Great Temptation, or the Great Blessing. For this power can drag man down until he is lower than the beast, or exalt him to the sky.

Man must prove his ability to use this power of creation wisely and well or learn thru its misuse the hard lesson gained in the suffering of sad experience.

Chapter 27 — The God of the Earth

Man is generally classed as an animal; a member of the animal kingdom. That classification is erroneous and misleading. It is the work of the church which makes a man a lowly, cringing creature in order to prepare his mind for the false doctrine it teaches of a god and a savior.

If man realized that he is the God of the Earth, he would know that he needs no other god and no saviour.

There is a vast, unbridgeable gulf between the lowest man and the highest animal. The animal remains in and never rises above its original status or its environment.

Such is not the case of man. Man is the master of himself, of his destiny, and of his environment. He wades into the wilderness and transforms it into a land of thriving cities, productive fields, fruit orchards, and citrus groves. He builds boats that sail over the waters of the sea and ships that fly through the air of space.

To place that Masterful Being on a low level with the beasts of the field is a serious error.

The Bible makes man the God of all the Earth, and the God of all creation, by definitely stating that he has dominion over all living things.

This status has a scientific foundation and is not a case of word-play nor euphemism. It is proven by the facts of biology, psychology, and metaphysics, and in many other ways. These facts show that man is the highest of all organized entities and the supreme being of all creation.

In the Pre-Existence of Man, he wrote: "Man is the God of his own being and his own existence. He has within himself the power or propagation and perpetuity. He can never become extinct. His pre-existence is plainly evident. Nor were these magic powers given to man or bestowed upon him by some imaginary god. They are an inherent part of him, of his very being, and cannot be given to him nor taken from him. Man has within himself all the potentialities of his own existences. He is the only true God. That God dwells in man and man in him, as the Bible says. And they are on the earth, not in the sky, not in 'that home above'."

The Bible clearly says, 'Know ye not that your body is the Temple of the Holy Ghost, which is you?. . .Know ye not that ye are the Temple of God and that the Spirit of God dwelleth in you? (1 Corinthians 3:16; 6:19). "No effort of concentration nor degree of reflection, no matter how long continued, can make man conscious of a personal identity in himself that is not himself -- that is separate from his body and distinct from his own brain. That fact is conclusive evidence to convince a rational mind that the Spirit of God, said to be dwelling in man's body, is none other than Man himself."

We should not ignore the truth nor disguise the plain facts in order to save the God of the church. Man is not an animal. He is a Divine Being in his own right. When we attempt to reduce him to the animal level, we create conditions of confusion that lead to many unsolvable complexities and erroneous conclusions.

Not only is man far above the animal level, but his State of Consciousness is high above that of all the animals; and that is largely what makes man a Divine Being.

By his own work, man has brought upon himself the degradation in which he wallows. He has violated practically every law of his being. He has eaten freely of the Forbidden Fruit, and the sad result was his "Fall" from his high estate, as related in symbol and allegory in the Bible.

By indulging in the sacred creative act on the animal level, and expending his Vital Essence in the function of propagation on the animal level, man has sunk to that level, and his State of Consciousness has also sunk to and corresponds with that low level.

This is the great mystery of life discovered by the Ancient Masters. By the expenditure and the dissipation of his Vital Essence in the creative act, performed mostly for pleasure and seldom for procreation, the result was a loss of certain Sense Powers, causing Man's State of Consciousness to fall from the high-god-plane of Seven to the low-animal-plane of five.

The Lamb of Revelation that looked like it had been sacrificed (Revelation 5:6) represents the trembling candidate who has been prepared, tried and tested for initiation in the Ancient Mysteries of Life, in the ritual of which we will be taught how to open those Seven Seals and the Book held in the right hand of him that sat on the throne (Revelation 5:1).

The activation of these Seven Seals forms the basic teachings of the Bible, heavily veiled in symbol and allegory, and misunderstood by the masses. That misunderstanding is purposely increased by priest and preacher, who declare that the Bible relates to its anthropomorphic God, and his son Jesus, and an imaginary heaven.

The vital importance of this great subject is the reason why the Bible is filled with teachings on Phallicism and why such teachings were always held most sacred by the Masters. They were always veiled from the masses in general, being revealed only to those whose purity of mind permitted them to grasp and appreciate the deeper truths of these teachings.

When man has conquered his body, when the Creative Fires of the Tree of Life are conserved, and have passed up thru the spinal cord, opened the Seven Seals of the body, and activated the Pituitary and Pineal Glands of the Brain, the Single Eye that fills the body with Light, man is then raised up, not from an earthly grave, but in his State of consciousness to the point where he can realize the Glory of the Lord and understand that he is that Lord of the Earth.